WESTERN Swing

The Life, Times & Music® Series

WESTERN Swing

The Life, Times & Music® Series

Andrew G. Hager

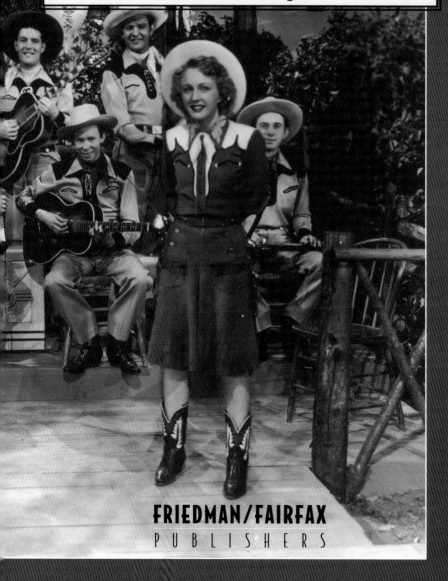

FRIEDMAN/FAIRFAX
PUBLISHERS

A FRIEDMAN/FAIRFAX BOOK

©1997 by Michael Friedman Publishing Group, Inc.

Library of Congress Cataloging-in-Publication Number 97-5486

ISBN 1–56799-506-3

Editor: Stephen Slaybaugh
Art Director: Jeff Batzli
Designer: Ruth Diamond
Photography Editor: Amy Talluto
Production Manager: Jeanne E. Hutter

Color separations by HK Scanner Arts Int'l Ltd.
Printed in Hong Kong by Midas Printing Limited.

For bulk purchases and special sales, please contact:
Friedman/Fairfax Publishers
15 West 26th Street
New York, NY 10010
(212) 685–6610 FAX (212) 685–1307

Visit our website: http://www.metrobooks.com

Dedication

To Sarah and Big Iron Skillet.

Acknowledgments

Special thanks to Steve Slaybaugh for his patience
and guidance, and to Nick Shaffran for his continuing
generosity in sharing his extensive knowledge
of country music.

Contents

Introduction   8

Milestones   10

Conception: The Light Crust Doughboys   12

Birth: Milton Brown and His Musical Brownies   18

Bob Wills and the Music's Growing Pains   29

The "King of Western Swing"   35

Into the Sunset   42

Western Bop   51

Recommended Listening   62

Bibliography   62

Index   63

Introduction

W hat has come to be known as western swing is a style of popular music borne by musicians of the lower Great Plains (predominately Texas and Oklahoma) in the decades preceding the Great Depression. Like all popular music of the United States, western swing came into existence because of the blending of many musical and cultural idioms.

The predominant root of the western swing sound is the string band. Until the rise of the first western swing band, Milton Brown and His Musical Brownies, bands of this specific region were generally made up of a fiddle or mandolin, a tenor guitar (a four-stringed instrument that is still popular among many Mexican musicians), and a standard six-string. Singers rarely performed with these ensembles before amplification since the human voice was inaudible over the din of dancers.

Though poor, the agrarian communities surrounding Fort Worth, Texas, did not go without entertainment. Folk who couldn't afford the price of dance hall admission or found taverns disreputable took turns sponsoring weekly house parties. By rolling up the rug, tossing cornmeal onto the floor, and alerting neighbors and their favorite musicians to a weekend's event, a family's living room could be converted into a dance hall.

Before the advent of radio and the record industry, most of the songs played at these gatherings were instrumental "breakdowns," a descendant of instrumental styles brought to the region by European settlers. Germans, who were the prominent ethnic group, as well as English, Irish, and French, added their own aesthetic to local music.

The first lacquer recordings pressed and distributed by northern entrepreneurs had an immediate and lasting impact on the Great Plains musicians. Songs and "licks" were no longer solely passed down among neighborhood musicians but were relayed between perfect strangers—whether they lived on the other side of the tracks from one another or thousands of miles apart.

Though many elements make up what we now call western swing, it was the incorporation of African-American musical styles at the beginning of the recording age that heralded its birth. Anglo musicians of the era have stated that their contact with blacks before the distribution of records and following the Civil War was extremely limited. And not until the rise of the turntable did Great Plains white musicians gain close enough musical contact with their black neighbors to acquire their techniques and thereby begin the creation of western swing.

While mass distribution served in some ways to break down regional, racial, ethnic, and religious barriers, it also began to build new ones through shortsighted marketing techniques and broad musical categorizations that were based on race and region. Records were labeled to clarify and simplify their marketing campaigns, a practice that ultimately led to stereotypes. The labeling of a record as "race" (i.e., African-American) or "hillbilly" prevented consumers, who refused to socialize or were forbidden from socializing with those outside their class and race, from buying a product whose contents were perceived as potential "dangers." Though the face, locale, and income of performers were forever removed from the recorded performance, the presumptions of a color-based and economic-caste society continued to be perpetuated. In the end, less units of certain recordings were sold.

An original member of the singing group the Sons of the Pioneers, Roy Rogers held a meeting of the most popular Hollywood cowboys to plan a museum in their honor. Of those pictured, Spade Cooley, Russ Hayden, Tennessee Ernie Ford, Bill Boyd, and Jimmy Wakely all came to the silver screen via western swing.

Milestones

Though at one time thousands of musicians and bandleaders practiced western swing in some fashion, only a handful of bands actually shaped the path that the rest simply followed. By the time the nation as a whole knew of western swing (and knew to call it by that name) the genre had passed its most decisive milestones. Thanks predominantly to the bands based in southern Oklahoma and northeastern Texas, the genre grew from the boundaries of its radio-confined region into an internationally recognized source of entertainment.

Thanks to mass production of records, regional music styles like western swing reached across their geographical boundaries to become a national craze.

Western swing evolved not only from musicians' exposure to new music through albums, but from the nature of early radio broadcasting. Since the early captains of the recording industry believed that sales of records would actually be hurt by airplay, broadcast music was performed live by local performers for nearly the duration of the golden age of radio. In this way, radio created a unique platform from which musicians and audiences explored, clarified, and codified their region's musical identity. The work of local performers was thereby self-legitimized. (The reverse holds true in today's internationally driven radio and recording market.)

Since stations couldn't sell their programs to listeners directly (airwaves were and remain free), financial backing via corporate sponsorship was a necessity, and radio began having another substantial impact on the boundaries of popular music. Because anyone young or old could turn on a radio, the music that companies were willing to sponsor was inherently limited (the sale of flour, for instance, was not necessarily best served by drinking

The success of "hillbilly" musical styles like western swing allowed entrepreneur/musician Chet Atkins to help build a vital music industry in Nashville, Tennessee.

songs). The nation's deeply ingrained impression of country music as family entertainment was formed from these relationships.

Conception: The Light Crust Doughboys

Though the Light Crust Doughboys (named by their radio sponsor Burris Mills) were a string—not a swing—band, its early members soon left this musical fold to put their stamp on the emerging lower Great Plains sound. The band remains intact to this day, though more as a novelty than as a continuing influence. In their heyday the Doughboys

The legendary Light Crust Doughboys pose for their first publicity shot: Bob Wills, Truett Kimzey (original KFJZ announcer), singer Milton Brown, and Herman Arnspiger.

Conception: The Light Crust Doughboys

Though the Light Crust Doughboys were not a western swing band in instrumentation or musical style, the founding fathers of that musical form began as members of this group. The band's second incarnation after the ouster of Milton Brown, from left to right: W. Lee O'Daniel, Bob Wills, Herman Arnspiger, Tommy Duncan, "Sleepy" Johnson, and driver Henry Steinbarth.

boasted the presence of western swing's forefathers as well as a future Texas governor, and an esteemed place in film history (the Doughboys were the first regional band to appear in a Hollywood movie).

By the mid-1920s, radio had quickly become the most powerful promotional tool for business. For those who involved themselves in the medium's infancy, emerging as a figure of local or statewide power was foreseeable and plausible. It is no wonder, then, that out of the six original members of the Light Crust Doughboys, three, plus several other later members of the band, hold a vital place in popular music history. Of the lauded collective who gained their place in the annals of music history, W. Lee "Pappy" O'Daniel wasn't even a musician.

It was obvious to most of the band's early listeners that Milton Brown (1903–1936) was, as a singularly talented

W. Lee O'Daniel (1890–1969)

A self-described poet/announcer, W. Lee O'Daniel involved himself heavily in the day-to-day operations of the Doughboys, a band he'd hired to promote Burris Mills products. When the band formed in 1930, the former Michigan resident had only recently acquired the company's seat of general management and placed a bet that radio would be a boon to business.

Though Truett Kimzey of KFJZ was the Doughboy's original announcer it was not long before O'Daniel, seeing that his bet had paid off, switched the band to radio station KTAT and appointed himself as their announcer. Until singer Milton Brown left the band, no one but O'Daniel was allowed to speak during the radio program. Within the first year of the Doughboys' radio stint, Burris Mills' profits increased by 150 percent.

O'Daniel's relationship with the Doughboys followed him for life. From those early days at Burris Mills to the building of his own flour company to a radio syndication conglomerate and ultimately to his governorship of the state of Texas, O'Daniel and his musicians stood side by side. His widely recognized voice, which has been described as paternalistic, would not have had its lifelong draw had it not been for the beautiful music and ever-growing reputation of the Doughboys. The image of a great entrepreneur trusted by good ol' folk like the members of the band led Texans to believe that O'Daniel was their worthy spokesman. Those who knew him closely, however, knew better. The portly O'Daniel often fed his band bananas instead of reasonable meals, kept the members' incomes consistently below the poverty line, and, after the sudden and tragic death of Milton Brown, campaigned for governor in Brown's hometown of Stephenville as one of the dearly departed's best friends. Milton's father posted notices throughout the town informing his neighbors otherwise.

Aware of the power that radio could afford him, W. Lee O'Daniel changed the Light Crust Doughboys show from KFJZ to KTAT radio station so that he could become the band's announcer.

Above: Originally of Michigan, W. Lee "Pappy" O'Daniel built a political and professional empire in Texas from his relationship with the founding musicians of western swing.

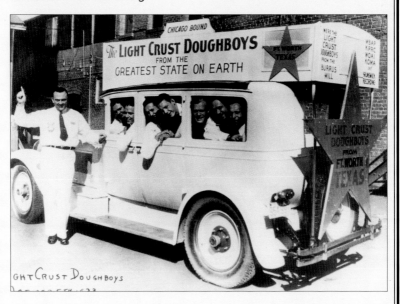

This is not to say that O'Daniel did nothing good for the state's residents. He did in fact push the legislature to give its poorest, oldest citizens a meager pension. He left the governor's office, though, with Texas $5 million in the hole and unable to raise revenues to pay for the pension he'd signed into law.

Above: W. Lee O' Daniel (left) and the Light Crust Doughboys prepare to go out on the road in 1933.

Two of the biggest influences on western swing: Jimmie Rodgers (left) and Roy Rogers.

singer, the reason that the Doughboys had become an overnight local sensation. Like the members of another Fort Worth–based band, the Southern Melody Boys, Brown helped bring instrumental improvisation to the local musical palette. Besides his singing, Milton also brought to the Doughboys the passionate rhythm guitar work of his younger brother Derwood, who worked for free through his teenage years.

Upon Derwood's graduation from high school in 1932, however, with his and Milton's father out of work due to illness, Milton asked O'Daniel to either give him a pay raise or to allow his brother to become a salaried member of the group. The boss denied both requests and Milton was forced to resign. In Brown's stead O'Daniel hired local singer Tommy Duncan (who is now the best-remembered singer of the western swing craze).

With Milton gone, the sound of the Doughboys changed drastically. Unlike Brown, Duncan was no crooner. His vocal style was more in line with "the Blue Yodeler," Jimmie Rodgers, who at the time was the most popular singer of hillbilly tunes (and is today considered the father of country music). Bob Wills (1905–1975), another original member of the Doughboys and a longtime friend of Brown, became the key to the band's successful transition.

Though a breakdown fiddler and unable to hold his own as a soloist, Wills' background in minstrelsy made him a real crowd pleaser. In the style of one of the era's most popular Anglo entertainers, Emmett Miller, Wills began doing comedic routines between sung numbers. O'Daniel obviously felt strong competition from the verbose Wills, and inevitably, trouble ensued. Their rivalry, which lasted for decades, ultimately landed the pair in court.

Jimmie Rodgers' blues-inflected, southern Anglo vocal style became the greatest influence on the male singers who spearheaded the western swing movement.

Birth: Milton Brown and His Musical Brownies

Directly following their departure from the Doughboys in 1932, Milton and Derwood Brown began assembling a band that was to be unrivaled for the next decade. It is only now, half a century after his contributions to the music, that quality research and a renewed interest in western swing have given Milton Brown and His Musical Brownies their rightful place as the originators of the genre.

Brown's command of vocal improvisation, reminiscent of Bing Crosby and Ukele Ike, was tempered by a deep appreciation for the voice of the father of country music, Jimmie Rodgers. By blending urbane vocal improvisational

Milton Brown and His Musical Brownies were the earliest and most influential western swing band. The Crystal Springs ballroom served as the home of the Brownies between circuitous Texas tours and is the acknowledged birthplace of western swing.

Birth: Milton Brown and His Musical Brownies

Milton returned to KTAT after forming the Brownies, becoming a successful rival of the Light Crust Doughboys. Members of Milton Brown and His Musical Brownies in 1933 from left to right: Wanna Coffman (bass), Marshal Pope (KTAT announcer), Milton Brown (vocals), Jesse Ashlock (fiddle), Fred "Papa" Calhoun (piano), Cecil Brower (fiddle), Ocie Stockard (banjo), and Derwood Brown (guitar).

dexterity with the tonal qualities of local music styles, Milton offered his listeners new sounds of the nation within a musical context that his neighbors could appreciate. Brown quickly became the most popular figure in northern Texas entertainment during the late 1920s and early 1930s.

Milton is also credited with the first of many reforms to the core instrumentation of string bands, which became the calling card of western swing bands to come. The inclusion of the upright bass, the piano, and the electrified pedal steel are all credited directly to Brown's direction of the Musical Brownies. The number of instruments used in western swing bands from that point forward continued to expand. By their heyday, western swing orchestras included a variety of diverse instrumentalists, from trumpeters to orchestral harpists.

Milton Brown and the Brownies pose for a radio publicity shot.

Dozens of western swing orchestras, some of which numbered thirty members, began replacing the jazz big band by the early 1940s in the dance halls of California, and by doing so heralded the decline of one uniquely American musical experience and the beginning of another.

Until the Brownies, the upright bass had rarely been used as part of the lower Great Plains string bands. In those cases where the bass was in fact used, as in Fort Worth's High Flyers, the instrument was bowed to accent the music's "pad," or key and chord pattern, rather than "slapped," a technique in which the fingers thump against the bass strings to give the instrument a role in the rhythm of the band.

The High Flyers

During their long career, the High Flyers helped not only to shape the sound of western swing but to keep it intact once the craze of the 1940s had wound down.

Al Stricklen, a pianist who was one of the group's founding members, said that within the band's first year together KFJZ began putting the High Flyers on the air three times a day under a variety of pseudonyms. Each night the group worked the Cinderella Roof in Dallas. Other founding members included Elmer Scarborough on banjo and tenor guitar; Willie Wells on bass, guitar, and vocals; Fred Dean on guitar; and Ocie Stockard, who would leave to join the Brownies, on banjo. In time the band incorporated Hardy "Jiggs" Harvey on sax, Homer Kinnard on drums, Pat Trotter on fiddle, and Landon Beaver, who took Stricklen's place after he left for Bob Wills' band.

The High Flyers first recorded in June 1937 and released seven records, including their popular song "A Little Green Mill." Out of the fourteen songs recorded, five were instrumentals and two featured a trio version of the band. Unfortunately the group disbanded later

that year for a brief period to work as soloists in different parts of the region. Elmer Scarborough and Willie Wells, specifically, left Texas for work at the famous XEPN radio station in Piedras Negras, Mexico.

Outside recording as a "pickup" group in 1938, the original High Flyers didn't re-form until 1939, when Oklahoma City and KOMA radio became their home base. Sleepy Johnson, of Doughboys and Milton Brown

Above: The High Flyers became one of the earliest bands to follow Milton Brown into the western swing genre.

fame, joined the group during this time. Unlike most of the recordings by western swing groups, the Flyers' first recording sessions after moving to Oklahoma (though recorded in Dallas) were self-penned tunes. By 1940 the band had found an entirely new sound by attaching a pick-up to the mandolin. The band's session in April of that year stands as the earliest example of electric mandolin on record.

Regretfully the High Flyers, like most bands of the era, broke up at the beginning of World War II and never again re-formed.

Left: With the rise of the western motion picture, the swing groups changed wardrobe to be more easily identifiable with fantasies of the Wild West.

Birth: Milton Brown and His Musical Brownies

At Milton's request, brother Derwood approached Wanna Coffman to play the bass for the Brownies. And although Coffman was excited by the offer to play with the locally popular Brown, he was shocked at Milton's request to play the "bass fiddle." Up until that time Coffman had only played tenor guitar. It was only hours after Derwood's offer that Coffman remembered that the tenor guitar and bass shared the same tuning and fingering. After months of practicing the "slap"—and with his fingers regularly

During the heyday of the Musical Brownies, the Crystal Springs ballroom served thousands of dancers a night. Built atop a natural aquifer, the club boasted a fresh springwater pool as well as Fort Worth's largest dance floor.

bleeding—Coffman became competent at the style and, by default, an innovator within string bands. In step with the Brownies' other rearrangements, the music as a whole in the region began to deemphasize the use of the tenor guitar and to rely on the percussive bass.

The use of songs in strict lyric form, as opposed to instrumental breakdowns, along with a focus on heavier rhythm took place inside the Brownies' collective. But it was the addition of the jazz piano stylings of Fred "Papa" Calhoun that caused the band to be categorically removed from that of a string band to western swing (though it was then termed a "string orchestra").

A student by proxy of Earl "Fatha" Hines (he listened incessantly to Hines' recordings), Calhoun was born in Chico, Texas, in 1904. By the age of sixteen he led a ten-piece jazz dance band made up primarily of horns. Originally a drummer, Calhoun moved to the piano when the pianist for his group left town. The inclusion of Dixieland barrelhouse piano—which in other parts of the country was called the stride school—remains a fixture within the southern and western string bands to this day.

Taking advantage of the disintegration of the acclaimed Southern

The Tune Wranglers

One of the earliest groups in the Fort Worth area to be purveyors of what would be called western swing was the Tune Wranglers, led by singer, guitarist, and songwriter Buster Coward. Unlike most musicians of the western swing era, the Tune Wranglers were made up of former cowhands who counted "breaking" horses among their favorite pastimes.

Beginning in 1935, fiddler Tom Dickey, bassist Charlie Gregg, and banjoist Eddie Fielding began playing the small town circuit of northeastern Texas. By 1936 the band had earned a spot on WOAI in San Antonio and began recording with Bluebird Records. Their first sides, which included their most popular song, "Texas Sand," were cut at the Texas Hotel in San Antonio on February 27 and 28.

That summer pianist Eddie Whitley, who'd only recently become a member of the band, quit to play with Jimmy Revard's Oklahoma Playboys, who'd gained popularity with their song "Let Me Live for You" (soon after they coerced Bob Wills into adding the word "Texas" to the name of his Playboys). George Timberlake, who'd worked with Revard and would do so again in the future, became the Wranglers' pianist. Eddie Duncan, a locally renowned steel player and singer, joined the group just in time for their October recording session. Buster was more comfortable singing blues numbers, while Duncan handled the pop songs. Sixteen sides were cut for the October 24, 1936, recording that gave the band their second success, "The One Rose in My Heart."

KTSA San Antonio began airing the Tune Wranglers to sponsor, of all things, Tune Wrangler coffee from the Plaza Hotel every afternoon. This gave the band time enough for out-of-town gigs, for which each musician averaged twenty dollars a performance—an enormous sum during the Depression.

Soon after their third recording session, which produced twelve sides, the Dickey Brothers—Tom and Bill (who'd only recently joined the group)—left to form their own band, Tom Dickey and the Showboys. Eddie Duncan also left for greener pastures.

The Wranglers, however, were at their all-time height of popularity. *Rural Radio* magazine in May 1938 said that the band traveled "more than 100,000 miles [160,900km] each year, in which time they visit over two hundred different towns. For transportation they require a new automobile each six months due to the constant traveling."

By 1938 the Wranglers were featuring twin fiddles, as was practiced first by the Southern Melody Boys and then the Brownies. Leonard Seago and Noah Hatley traded fiddle licks while new editions the Ruff twins, Beal (sax and clarinet) and Neal (banjo), added their own unique offerings to western swing. Their final sessions came in October of that year, with Duncan having returned to take the place of Noah Hatley. Hawaiian numbers played a large role in the recording, mostly instrumentals, including their last fan favorite, "Hawaiian Honeymoon."

The Tune Wranglers continued at full pace for the next two years until World War II tore the band apart. In the interim Buster Coward and Tom Dickey died, and Bill Dickey retired to Kingland, Texas. Charlie Poss, who spent a time at keyboards for the band, went on to hammer at the ivories in San Antonio for the unstoppable Adolph Hofner.

RCA VICTOR
For best results use
RCA Victor Needles
20-2070-B
TEXAS SAND
The Tune Wranglers
Singing with orchestra

Birth: Milton Brown and His Musical Brownies

Bob Wills and the Texas Playboys began their ascent to national stardom once Wills was released from the army and resettled in Los Angeles. The continual addition of new instruments like the trumpet, to western swing, pit Wills against the leaders of the jazz big bands.

Melody Boys, Milton filled out his ensemble with the addition of another fiddler to play along with cofounder Jesse Ashlock. Cecil Brower, unlike Ashlock, was a trained musician with a vast knowledge of chord progressions and tonal relativity.

The Southern Melody Boys, with Brower and Kenneth Pitts on dueling fiddles, was the first group with a capacity for instrumental improvisation in 1931. The incorporation of instrumental solos proved to be a cornerstone of western swing as Brown allowed the musicians around him the freedom to fully explore their own improvisational voices within the string band. With the inclusion of Brower, the band now had three soloists: a fiddler, the singer, and the pianist.

Last but far from least of the innovations put into motion by the Brownies was the inclusion of an instrument as yet unheard of—the electrified lap steel. Bob Dunn was not only the beast's inventor but a gifted player whose sole passion was his instrument. Also a notorious drinker and transient, Dunn showed up to play with the band for the first time in clothes so tattered that Milton immediately bought him a new suit (Dunn apparently got himself together in his later years, receiving a degree in music and owning his own music store in Houston, Texas).

No matter where the Brownies played, a crowd was sure to gather. Each member of the band made about sixty dollars a night for his effort—an amazing sum in the midst of the Great Depression. Imagine a local band so successful that each member drove a brand new car. So popular was Milton Brown personally that at his funeral a line of cars three thousand long followed the hearse from services in Fort Worth back to his hometown of Stephenville, where he was laid to rest. Brown's eighteen-year-old wife, who'd only recently borne his child, Buster, at the time of Milton's death (and even more recently had divorced him), kept Brown's last name for the rest of her life though she remarried several times (twice to Bob Wills).

Before his death, Milton had foreseen a bright future for western swing. His reputation had spread farther and

Birth: Milton Brown and His Musical Brownies

Adolph Hofner (b. 1916)

Out of all the original band leaders of the western swing era only one, Adolph Hofner, is still going strong. The San Antonio resident can still be found, along with his band's pianist, Al Stricklen (formerly of the Texas Playboys), pumping out swinging tunes—some fifty years after his entrance into the forum.

As with many Texas bands of the early thirties, Hofner's participation in western swing didn't occur until Milton Brown and His Musical Brownies had hit the scene. From that moment forward, however, Adolph Hofner was, in his own words, "a confirmed hillbilly."

Following the trend of many Texas swing performers, Adolph Hofner moved his band to California following World War II. There he began recording for Columbia records. Pictured is an album from that period reissued by Arhoolie.

Adolph Hofner and His San Antonians have practiced western swing longer than any other group of the genre.

Hofner's band, the San Antonians, began with members Floyd Tillman (who later in life became a renowned songwriter), Adolph's brother Emil, Chet Carnes, Leonard Seago (of the Tune Wranglers), and Bert Ferguson. RCA/Bluebird began recording the San Antonians, though with a pickup staff of musicians, in 1937.

By World War II, the group, one member at a time, began leaving for the service. Hofner picked up replacements including Eddie Duncan of the Tune Wranglers and Leonard Brown. As fiddlers became more scarce Hofner began including horn players to the band, which turned out to delight his loyal following.

Adolph and the San Antonians moved to California in 1945 and worked for the following two years on the Foreman Phillips County Barn Dances. Columbia became their label and noteworthy songs like "Alamo Rag" and "Sagebrush Shuffle" were recorded. Texas beckoned the band back, and since 1949 the group has been sponsored by Texas' own Pearl Beer and been known as the Pearl Wranglers.

Almost fifty years later the band still maintains a steady schedule, playing four to five nights a week. The band's staff at one time included both of Adolph's daughters, Kathy and Darlene, as singers and drummers.

farther across midwestern America. He'd been approached by Republic Pictures to be the first regional star of the movies. It had become obvious to everyone including Brown that his style of music, whether led by him or someone else, was going to be the next great craze.

But the sacrifices asked of him had taken their toll. The last publicity photo of the dapper Milton Brown—the man known for his urbane nature and fancy cars—was of Milton in a ten-gallon hat looking exhausted as hell and, for the first time ever, without his trademark smile.

Brown was a great fan of early jazz and, though born in the tiny town of Stephenville, Texas, saw himself in the likeness of his urban jazz contemporaries. In no way was the music that the Brownies performed perceivably "hillbilly."

Local Fort Worth press, in fact, described the band as a well-dressed string orchestra, bringing to light the community's vision of the group as a refined extension of their folk tradition. It wasn't until the northern recording companies planted satellite offices in Dallas and San Antonio that Milton Brown, along with his regional peers, were effectively tagged hillbillies.

Bob Wills and the Music's Growing Pains

Many western swing legends, including Bob Wills, emerged from behind the shadow of Milton Brown. Long before the Doughboys and the Brownies—and well before

After nearly a decade of struggling to make a healthy living as a musician, Bob Wills became one of the dominant western swing bandleaders of the forties.

Bob Wills' success on the California Western Swing scene made him an ideal candidate for the silver screen, though his work in film never gained a sizeable audience like that of Gene Autry, Roy Rogers, and Bill Boyd.

the arrival of Wills—Barty Brown and his sons, Milton and Derwood, entertained their Fort Worth neighbors. When Wills and musicians like him came through Fort Worth, the Browns were the folk they paid a visit to.

A Texan by birth but Oklahoman by upbringing, James Robert Wills was a husband and father and in need of work by the time he arrived in Fort Worth. Though Fort Worth was nearly a city by that time, it was still dependent upon an agrarian economy. But in his own mind Wills couldn't or wouldn't see himself finding work as a farmhand or grain elevator operator once in town. He risked everything—from his family to food and lodging—to be a full-time musician. Throughout the first half of his life, Wills would at least once lose each of these precious things.

Wills' first steady work in Fort Worth came with his inclusion in Brown's first band, the Aladdin Laddies, which soon became the Doughboys. From 1930 to 1932 the group gained tremendous local success.

After Milton was forced to leave the band in search of financially greener pastures, Wills and Tommy Duncan were left in charge of reshaping the Doughboys' sound by making the best use of the talent left within the band. A musical gap was evident with Brown's departure and couldn't simply be refilled. Milton was an innovator whose voice alone had changed their community's perspective on popular singing.

The Texas Playboys, along with Spade Cooley's orchestra, took over the large ballrooms of the West Coast that were, before their arrival, homes to jazz bands.

Bill Boyd and the Cowboy Ramblers

Next to Bob Wills, Bill Boyd (1910–1977) is one of the most enduring legends of western swing. Thanks to his catchy instrumentals— "Under the Double Eagle," "New Fort Worth

A favorite of parents and kids alike, singer-turned-actor Bill Boyd always had time for autographs.

Rag," "New Spanish Two Step," and "Roadside Rag"—Boyd has been called the "King of the Instrumentals" by such historians as Tom Dunbar. Together with his brother Jim (b.1914), Boyd built an illustrious career from virtually nothing.

The duo was raised, along with their eleven brothers and sisters, on a 320-acre (128ha) cattle ranch and cotton farm in Fannin Country, Texas. Music was constantly present in the Boyd household, with both parents always singing and tunes from around the nation ringing from the family Victrola.

KFPM in Greenville, Texas, gave Bill and Jim (sixteen and twelve years old, respectively), along with their neighbors Howard and Bill Staley, their first opportunity to perform, in 1926. Though the brothers Boyd knew from

that point forward that music was their calling, the sudden death of their father kept them ranch-bound for another three years. However, with diminishing profits in cattle and cotton at the beginning of the Depression, the Boyds sold the family property in 1929 and moved to Dallas.

While Bill took whatever work he could find, from roofing to delivery service, Jim began studying at Dallas Technical High School. Soon after, Jim met Audrey "Art" Davis, who played fiddle, mandolin, and clarinet, and for the next three years Art and Jim played at a variety of school functions.

Their first stroke of good luck came in 1932 when Bill and O. P. Alexander, along with their friend Red Stevens, landed work on an early-morning WFAA radio program. For the next two years the trio played their unique combination of guitar, french harp, and mandolin, gaining local success.

Once Jim was finished with school in 1932, the brothers formed a four-piece band called the Cowboy Ramblers. Much like the other string bands in the burgeoning western swing movement, the Ramblers soon acquired a variety of other musicians and grew substantially in size.

In August 1934 the band began their first recordings with Bill on guitar, Jim on bass, Art Davis on fiddle, and Walter Kirkes on tenor banjo. "The Ramblers' Rag" and "I'm Gonna Hop Off the Train" both emerged from this session.

Beginning in 1936 the Cowboy Ramblers cut nearly 230 sides for RCA Records. Thanks to the success of their first big hit with Bluebird, "Under the Double Eagle," the personnel for the band, though relatively the same on the road, expanded to include per-

Bill Boyd and the Cowboy Ramblers of 1946: Billy Jack Saucier, violin; Cleo Hoyt, accordion; brother Clyde Boyd, drums; Fred Casers, bass; Bill Boyd, Jake Wright, and brother Jim Boyd, guitars; and Bill Osborne, pedal steel.

formers from a variety of successful bands. Jesse Ashlock, who had first played with Milton Brown and spent most of his career with Bob Wills, was counted among the Ramblers. In addition, Cecil Brower and Fred Calhoun, other Brownie alumni; Kenneth Pitts and Milton Montgomery, both Doughboys; and younger brother John Boyd were all at one time recording with Bill and Jim. From their extensive sessions with these musicians came many a popular tune. "Goofus," "Beaumont Rag," "Palace in Dallas," and "Over the Wave Waltz" are counted among their fans' favorites.

While many American men were abroad during World War II, Bill Boyd began his movie career. Thanks to his manager Jack Adams, who was also a film distributor and Producers Releasing Corporation franchise holder, Bill became a leading man nearly overnight, starring in six feature films, including *Tumbleweed Trail* and *Along the Sundown Trail*. Many of the films costarred Art Davis, who'd left the Ramblers in 1938 to work with Gene Autry. In an effort to do his part for the war effort, Bill also began entertaining servicemen and appearing in shows to promote the sale of war bonds.

His work as a star, promoting his movies and the songs therein, continued until after the war when Bill reunited with his brother Jim to re-form the Cowboy Ramblers. Until the mid-1950s the duo and their sidemen continued to keep their end of western swing alive.

Like many of the western swing stars, Bill Boyd had his turn as a hero of the silver screen.

Bob Wills and the Music's Growing Pains

Wills' long years spent on the medicine show circuit had honed his ability to play to a crowd; his superior timing and ability to deliver a lyric or punchline were perhaps his greatest assets. Many within Fort Worth felt that with Brown's departure the Doughboys were as good as finished. But when Wills stepped up to the microphone to do his routine, the band became a real contender against the new radio show featuring expatriate Brown.

But the vain O'Daniel, though relieved that the show had not outright failed with the departure of the Brown brothers, wasn't happy for long with Wills at the microphone. There could only be one voice of the popular Doughboys and it certainly wasn't going to be Wills for long. O'Daniel had bought and paid for the podium. After months of feuding, Wills left to form his own band.

Unfortunately, Wills wasn't as lucky as Milton upon his sudden and blustery departure from the Light Crust Doughboys. There were already two successful bands in Fort Worth and the town probably couldn't afford a third. With band in tow, Wills made a move to Waco, the next-biggest town southeast of Fort Worth. Unfortunately the radio station, WACO, had a very limited broadcast range and Wills, in turn, had little publicity for himself or his band's weekly club dates.

Milton Brown did everything he could to help out his old friend, even planning double bills around Waco. Though Wills gained exposure for his band at these events, it was obvious that the crowds came out to see the Brownies, rarely returning to see Wills at his own showcase events.

Once again Bob and company packed up and moved, first to Oklahoma City, and then, when things turned out to be as fruitless there as in Texas, they quickly moved to Tulsa. From 1934 to 1942 Wills and the Texas Playboys played daily at radio station KVOO. In 1935 they began recording with Okeh Records, and after the death of Milton Brown in 1936, Bob Wills and the Texas Playboys became the most popular band in the Southwest.

By 1941, however, competition was getting stiff out West. Though Wills and Duncan's recording of "New San Antone Rose" had spread the band's name across the country, the western swing movement in California was fueling western films. Still widely acclaimed today as the leader of western swing's heyday of the 1940s, Bob Wills along with his Texas Playboys faced heavy competition from another native Oklahoman named Spade Cooley.

The "King of Western Swing"

Spade Cooley (1910-1969) was the host of television's longest running show, the most popular entertainer west of the Mississippi, the leader of America's largest big band, the owner of a twenty-acre (8 ha) estate on Ventura Boulevard in Los Angeles, and held assets worth $15 million by 1961.

Because he murdered his wife, Clyde Donnell "Spade" Cooley, the once "King of Western Swing," is often overlooked.

The Spade Cooley orchestra, at one time the most popular band on the West Coast, boasted thirty-two musicians, including a harpist.

Besides being able to boast the largest of bands, Spade is cited as the man who coined the term "western swing." Until the early forties the music had been called a number of names, from the overused term hillbilly to Texas swing.

So why has his legacy been lost in only a matter of forty years? It seems America has a short memory for musical heroes turned murderers. At the peak of his financial success, Clyde Donnell Cooley, on April 3, 1961, forced his daughter to watch as he murdered his second wife and former singer Ella Mae Evans. The defendant at the first "Trial of the Century," the "King of Western Swing" spent the rest of his life behind bars. Eerily enough, "Crazy 'Cause I Love You," "Shame on You," and "You Clobbered Me" (sung by his female star and wife) were all popularized by Spade Cooley and His Orchestra. With Cooley's demise, Bob Wills took over the title of King of Western Swing.

Born in a storm cellar near Pack Saddle Creek, Oklahoma, on December 17, 1910, Spade often described himself as "born poor and raised poor." As the son of migrant workers and a student at an Indian public school

Roy Rogers played a pivotal role in Cooley's life—twice. First, he gave Spade his professional break, and then he supposedly drove Spade to murder by having an affair with his wife.

After the success of his live performances, Cooley ventured into radio, television, and film. Cooley made two short films for RKO that spotlighted his orchestra.

he was able to "pass" for Caucasian. But like African-American mulattos and octoroons, "Spade" was to be considered by law an Indian no matter how little (one quarter) Native American blood coursed through his veins.

Thanks to good luck and an affinity for risk, however, Cooley quickly learned how the desperately poor are able to get ahead. A penchant for gambling brought him his nickname and, ultimately, overwhelming success. For the first third of his life, however, Cooley was barely able to make ends meet for himself, his Native American first wife, and their son.

Down on his luck in the City of Angels, Spade waited outside Republic Pictures' studio for Roy Rogers. He'd heard of Rogers' reputation for kindness and generosity and knew that if given the chance he could convince Rogers to give him a job. The introduction finally came, and though Spade had likely hoped for work as an actor or musician, Rogers offered him a job as his body double.

During the day Spade took on-camera beatings for Rogers and at night worked wherever he could as a fiddle player. Cooley became so in demand among local bands that the manager of the Venice Pier Ballroom told him that he should start his own band. Cooley took his advice and within only a few months was a headlining act.

Spade Cooley and His Orchestra became so phenomenally popular that Spade decided to lease his own club: the eight-thousand-square-foot (744 sq m) Riverside Rancho. However, the club soon proved too small for the crowds that gathered and the Santa Monica Ballroom soon became the band's home.

Meanwhile, Spade's personal life had begun to show seams. His first wife had filed for divorce and obtained custody of their son, John. And at nearly the same time Ella Mae Evans, Cooley's future wife, became the female vocalist for the band.

To keep ahead of the musical curve, Spade was constantly adding new dimensions to his band. And by 1946 he had begun incorporating new rhythms into western swing while playing at the Santa Monica Ballroom. The blues, the rhumba, and boogie-woogie were all integral parts of Cooley's heavy backbeat.

By 1960 Spade had achieved more success than any

The Western Caravan

In 1946 a handful of former members of the most popular band in western swing, Spade Cooley's orchestra, left to form their own band. The Western Caravan, though led onstage by Tex Williams (1917–1985), was a collective operation with members taking on the various daily duties of the business.

Thanks primarily to the band's tremendous success with Spade's organization, the band began performing directly upon formation. The roller rink on Glendale Boulevard in Los Angeles drew a substantial crowd every weeknight and was packed to capacity on the weekends.

The Caravan prided itself on its commitment to "traditional" western swing and chose to stick primarily with string players. The band boasted three European-style violinists, a stride pianist à la Earl Hines, and three vocalists, each of whom specialized in different styles of song (pop, country, and ballad). Comedic sketches were also part of the evening's entertainment, between and during songs, thanks to singers Smokey Rogers and Deuce Spriggins.

Recording for Capitol Records began almost immediately but it was two years before the band had an enormously successful single. "Smoke, Smoke, Smoke (That Cigarette)" went to the top of both the pop and country charts in 1947 and earned the group a platinum record.

Concerned that Cooley was drifting from his roots in hillbilly music, Tex Williams and fellow bandmembers left Spade's fold to start their own band, the extremely popular Western Caravan.

other person in western swing. His television show had been on for over a decade, and he had starred in several films and scored music for many others. Never satisfied, Cooley started developing plans for Water Wonderland, an amusement park to be carved out of the Mojave Desert. Three lakes were planned, the property had been bought, and blueprints for everything from a western town to a twenty-thousand-square-foot (1,860 sq m) dance hall with television broadcasting facilities were in place. But right before the digging of the first lake, Spade was arrested on a charge of murder and his daughter became the star witness against him.

Though he had the finest lawyer money could buy, nothing could sway the jury from the heartwrenching testimony of his daughter. He was found guilty and sentenced to twenty-five years in prison. After serving only eight and a half of those years, Spade was scheduled for release. Just before the end of his stretch, following a performance for the league of prison guards, Spade Cooley died from his fourth heart attack.

By the time Wills arrived on the West Coast, Cooley was one of the most popular western band figures leading the largest orchestra in all the land. Once again Wills was (if he was lucky) number two on the totem pole.

Cooley and Wills shared the stage in double band billings (at Cooley's club) much like Bob had with Milton a decade before. Thankfully the audience for the music had grown considerably and could embrace two kings of western swing.

Into the Sunset

The West, a mythical wilderness where wealth awaited those who survived the treacherous journey to the Pacific, proved fertile ground for the imaginations of consumers and in turn for the pocketbooks of performers who were willing to participate in the propagation of its mystique. Though the West was fully explored by the 1940s and its prairies effectively cordoned off by barbed wire, images of cowboys on the open range continued to be evoked.

Left to right, Tex Williams, Eddie Dean, and Kathy Marlowe sport duds fashioned by cowboy clothes designer Norman Nudie of Hollywood.

Some western swing musicians like Bill Boyd, consciously played to the perception of their audiences by dressing in the cowboy garb of their film counterparts.

Thanks to motion pictures, for which Milton Brown was going to be the first regional music star before he died unexpectedly in 1936, entertainers displayed not only their voice but their physical image. Fringed costumes, ornate boots, and seemingly weatherproof cowboy hats became standard issue thanks to the transition from radio to film. The western musicians who were most successful during the golden age of the 1930s and 1940s consciously played to the misconceptions of their cinema-crazed audience rather than nobly and profitlessly trying to educate them about the history of the West. The plots were far from remi-

Hank Thompson and His Brazos Valley Boys

A native of Waco, Texas, and a former member of the Light Crust Doughboys, Hank Thompson (b. 1925) was cut from the same material as his western swing predecessors. The music of his hometown was kept alive and well for more than twenty-five years past the golden age of western swing thanks to Hank Thompson and His Brazos Valley Boys.

Thompson spent his high school years playing a four-dollar guitar that his mother had bought him, and eventually landed a spot on WACO radio as "Hank the Hired Hand." Between semesters at the University of Texas and Southern Methodist University, Thomson moved back home to continue singing professionally on local radio. Globe Records of Dallas asked him to record for them, and with the Brazos Valley Boys, Hank cut two original tunes, "Swing Wide Your Gate of Love" and "Whoa, Sailor," both of which became local hits. With the help of an admirer—none other than singing cowboy Tex Ritter—the band got a contract with Capitol Records. For the next two decades Thompson recorded hit after hit, including "Today" and "Humpty-Dumpty Heart."

Of his seventy-nine hit songs, probably the most well remembered is "The Wild Side of Life." Although the song went to number one and stayed on the charts for fifteen weeks, it is probably best remembered for Kitty Wells' response to the song's message, "It Wasn't God Who Made Honky Tonk Angels," which attempted to give the female perspective on the wayward women that Thompson raved about in "Wild Side." Wells and her husband, Johnnie Wright, would share the spotlight on Thompson's "Six Pack to Go." The tune by the threesome went to number ten on the *Billboard* charts.

Hank Thompson, formerly of the Light Crust Doughboys, made a healthy living from the music and costumes of western swing long after the music's golden age had come and gone.

niscent of the Great Plains performers' lives back home, and the costumes were obviously nicer than the tattered duds of sharecroppers, which many of them had at one time worn.

However, like the jazz bands that Wills and his protégés once replaced, western swing was destined to fade from popularity as were the stars of western films. America's growing urban culture shared few similarities to the Wild West and successful new urban music strategies began making stars of the former jazz big band frontpersons. Torch singers like Dinah Shore, Doris Day, and Frank Sinatra effectively stole the limelight away from the likes of Roy Rogers and Dale Evans and by doing so forced the western and southern music business to face economic downsizing and a second-place position (if that) in the hearts of Americans.

Although it was merely a dream until the late 1940s, recording entrepreneurs began building an empire—a single center for rural music—from Nashville's successful Grand Ole Opry radio program. Though it seems to music fans today that Nashville has forever been the cutting edge of rural music, the city's first records weren't actually pressed until the late 1940s, around the same time that *Billboard* magazine changed their classification of the music from "hillbilly" to "country."

At the helm of the emerging empire was a handful of producers determined to make use of all the current recording techniques, equipment, and popular styles of arrangement. Of these early producers Chet Atkins (b. 1924) is no doubt the best remembered and most successful. A jazz guitarist by training, Atkins worked to develop the Nashville Sound

Like western swing performers before him, Chet Atkins blended jazz and country music, but with a different outcome. From his experiment the Nashville Sound was born.

and by doing so helped distance the music from the often primitive sounds of "hillbilly" recordings.

As always, the western and now country tunes that became most widely known were from the pens of professional songwriters, many of whom worked in Tin Pan Alley (Manhattan's former music publishing district). To co-opt the Big Apple's hold on crafty songs, producers in Nashville began building their own stable of songwriters that soon rivaled and now outshines the East Coast's.

In the same way that images used in rural music of the late twenties changed from Appalachian to western, lyrics again underwent a metamorphosis following the decline of

As a former Fort Worth resident, Ernest Tubb was steeped in the western swing tradition. Like the western swing innovators before him, Tubb incorporated a new instrument into "hillbilly" music—the electric guitar. Tubb is also credited with changing the name of the music from "hillbilly" to "country."

Hank Thompson and His Brazos Valley Boys kept western swing alive nearly sin-gle-handedly for the two decades that followed the form's heyday. All told, Thompson and his band accrued seventy-nine hit songs.

the western craze. Though their tunes were similar (and sometimes identical) to songs of the western swing bands, the lyrics emerged from their surgery without a trace of horse or prairie.

Some of the most popular musicians who gained fame after the transition to the Nashville Sound remained true to the ideals and ornamentation, in one way or another, of western swing. Ernest Tubb (1914–1984) continued in the western tradition of dress by donning bright yellow kerchiefs, green western-style suits, and a cowboy hat. As a former Fort Worth resident, Tubb was not only aware of but in fact steeped in the western swing tradition. And like other western innovators Tubb incorporated a new instrument into the rural tradition. The electric guitar, his pride and joy, lent a signature sound to Tubb's priceless laid-back tunes.

Another Texan, Hank Thompson, followed more closely than Tubb in the costumes and storytelling devices of the western tradition. A Light Crust Doughboy band alumnus, Thompson grew up idolizing Bob Wills. In full cowboy garb Thompson and His Brazos Valley Boys remained popular with country audiences for nearly two decades and garnered seventy-nine hit songs. When looking back at pictures of Thompson from the late 1950s it's hard to imagine that they weren't taken some twenty years earlier, revealing the "retro" nature of his stage persona.

Outside western swing disciples, a new breed of performers arose. As the name implies, the honky-tonk music of the 1940s and 1950s suited the needs of roadhouse patrons. Notoriously rowdy, the average honky-tonk club boasted dancing, heavy drinking, and fighting, which put serious demands on their road-weary entertainers. Unlike the rhythmic underpinnings of the western big band, the booming honky-tonk sound came from a group of no more than six musicians. And though the new public announcement (P.A.) systems gave them a slight advantage in volume over the crowd, the music itself underwent an energetic boost. Honky-tonk's popular frontmen—the two most successful being Hank Williams and Lefty Frizzell—gained the attention of the average savage with dynamic stage presences and commanding vocals.

Throughout the twentieth century, every new decade seemed to demand a complete reconfiguring of the American cultural musical equation. As quickly as honky tonk had arrived on the scene, an entirely new style of music began warming up in the wings. The heavy bass and locomotive rhythms that the leaders of western swing had first incorporated and the performers of honky tonk had reinvigorated were again bolstered by the mid- to late fifties as white teenagers sought their own brand of music.

Bill Haley began his career as a country singer and yodeler but became one of the first of a handful of performers to be labeled a western bopper. The music eventually came to be known as rock and roll.

Western Bop

Although the music that teenagers of the era embraced was shocking to the majority of parents, it did not arrive without warning. The western bop movement (as the style of music was first called) was influenced by the music of past generations. It was a reasonable, albeit hyperactive, extension of twentieth-century Anglo-American folk music, and as had been true of popular music since the beginning of the recording age, the style's changes were based on a reconfiguration of key American cultural elements. The

Bill Haley recorded "Shake Rattle and Roll," which was also a hit for another star originally labeled western bop: Elvis Presley.

influence of African-American rhythms and the energy of popular black performers gained more acceptance than ever during the era in white string bands. As the name attests, western bop bowed to the roots of western swing and to the most recent genre of popular African-American music, bebop. The title, however, didn't stick. Within five years after the first white western bop performers (some referred to them as rockabillys) came on the scene, the music became known as rock and roll.

The first popular performer to be hailed a western bopper was Michigan resident and former country singer/yodeler Bill Haley (1925–1981). He and his group the Saddlemen (soon after renamed the Comets) recorded the groundbreaking "Rocket 88" in 1951, a full eight years before most of the rock and roll royalty broke onto the scene. And although inspired by the raucous radio talk of deejay Alan Freed, "Rock Around the Clock" became an anthem for the new style in 1954—a full year before Freed used the term "rock 'n' roll" to promote his national music tours.

Lubbock, Texas, legend Buddy Holly and the king of rock and roll, Elvis Presley, also began their careers (or so the promotional copy read) as performers of western bop. But popular consensus finally converted the industry's marketing needs and they referred to the musicians as purveyors of rock and roll. Though the music was actually a link in the lineage of the music of formerly popular figures like Brown and Wills, a revolution was afoot. A gap between the young and old began to take shape and rock and roll was the wedge between the generations.

Navigating the historical terrain for evidence of western swing's influence in rock and roll from that point forward gets hazy, though clear glimpses appear on the peripheries, in acoustic rock groups of the 1960s folk movement, in acts like rockabilly revivalists the Stray Cats, and in the

Although there wasn't anything "western" about his appearance, Lubbock, Texas native Buddy Holly was influenced by the western swing sound.

1990s arrangements and singing style of Dave Matthews. But the most apparent path of western swing's influence since the rise and realignment of western bop is most easily traced through the musicians of country music.

A third resurgence in western swing interest came with the rise of Austin, Texas, as a music mecca of the early 1970s. Though Austin musicians like Waylon Jennings and Willie Nelson (b. 1933) felt no need to reawaken the fashion sense of Wills and his protégés, they did share their musi-

Willie Nelson's passion for western swing was kindled at an early age. As a teenager Nelson booked Bob Wills and His Texas Playboys to play his tiny hometown of Abbot, Texas.

A life-long fan of western swing, Merle Haggard was named Top Male Vocalist and Entertainer of the Year by the Academy of Country and Western Music in 1971. Here he poses with his awards with composer Henri Mancini and singer Lanie Kazan, two of the event's presenters.

cianship and aesthetic sensibility. As a teenager Nelson was such a fan of Wills that he booked the band himself to play his tiny hometown of Abbot, Texas. The music he heard that special night must have fine-tuned his appreciation for the Mexican ballad and the polka as well as jazz arrangements and improvisation.

Every musician who made his way to Austin during the seventies seemed to have an affinity for western swing. By removing themselves from the often strange, extraneous rigors of Nashville and rejoicing in, rather than renouncing, the history of twentieth-century "hillbilly" music, these

Merle Haggard (b. 1937)

Now an institution in country music, Merle Haggard performed a world-wide televised concert on Austin City Limits in 1996.

Merle Haggard has always shared a great deal in common with the stars of western swing. Like many who had migrated from Oklahoma, Haggard found music to be his greatest friend in hard times (of which he's had his fair share). With his band The Strangers he put together a tribute to the work of Bob Wills in the early eighties, and from that retrospective album came the number one hit "I Think I'll Just Stay Here and Drink."

Although born in Oklahoma, "the Hag" spent his early years in Bakersfield, California, where he and his family spent several years call-ing a refrigeration railroad car at a "Hoover Camp" home.

When Merle was nine years old, his father, a fiddle-playing sharecropper, died of a stroke, leaving the Haggard family to fend for themselves. Haggard's childhood and teenage years were spent scraping together enough cash to stay alive. At the age of fourteen, Haggard was booked on suspicion of armed robbery and in 1957 went to San Quentin for breaking and entering. Haggard was released a few days before his twenty-third birthday after serving two and a half years of a one-to-fifteen sentence.

In 1963 Haggard had his first top twenty hit, "Sing a Sad Song," at the same time he began his descent into heavy drinking and cocaine use. He soon divorced his wife Leona and quickly married Bonnie Owens (Buck's ex-wife).

The year 1965 brought Haggard's first top ten hit, "All My Friends Are Gonna Be Strangers," and an award from the Association of Country Music (ACM) for Top New Male Vocalist. However, it wasn't until two years later that Merle had his first number one hit, "I'm a Lonesome Fugitive." "Okie from Muskogee," the first of several of his million-selling singles, was released in 1971 from the album *Fightin' Side.*

In 1972 Ronald Reagan, then the governor of California, officially pardoned Haggard. The pardon now hangs in the Country Music Hall of Fame.

After ten years of marriage, Bonnie, who continues to sing backup for Merle, decided she could no longer stand his cocaine abuse and divorced him. His third wife, also named Leona (Williams), was able to stay married to him for five years; his fourth wife, Debbie Parrett, stuck around only long enough to force him into drug treatment. No doubt tired of the paperwork, Merle has not married his most recent love, Theresa, who is the mother of his daughter, Jenessa, born December 23, 1989.

All told, Haggard has been honored as Male Vocalist of the Year nine times by the Academy of Country Music (ACM), the Country Music Association (CMA), and Music City News (MCN) collectively; was named Entertainer of the Year in 1970 by both the ACM and CMA; and received honors for Songwriter of the Year from MCN in that same year. He and former wife Bonnie have won three duet awards while he and Willie Nelson have also taken home CMA's Vocal Duo of the Year award.

A legend bows to his mentor: Merle Haggard's A Tribute to the Best Damn Fiddle Player in the World (or, My Salute to Bob Wills).

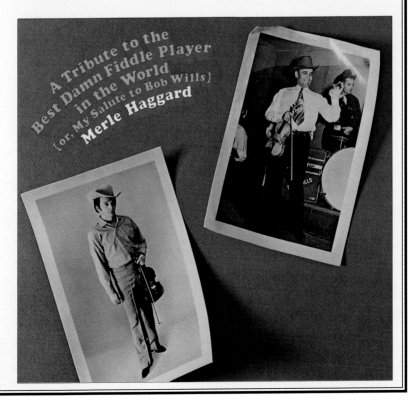

Two of the day's greatest country singers, Merle Haggard and Willie Nelson, share top honors. The Country Music Association awarded them Vocal Duo of the Year in 1983 for the song and album, "Poncho and Lefty."

musicians claimed the music of Texas for Texans. Though the Austin scene seemed to fade during the eighties (and then reemerge, at least as an industry, thanks to the annual South by Southwest music and multimedia festival), the relationship between today's country music and its roots in western swing has spread into a national, often nostalgically driven, phenomenon.

In the late 1980s a band who'd been popular in Austin's heyday in the 1970's, Asleep at the Wheel, again found the spotlight with their covering of western swing tunes, in fact playing with the old-timers of western swing on television's *Austin City Limits.*

Many players who are not so bent on nostalgia revisit western swing with great regularity. Virtuosic mandolin player Ricky Skaggs always laces an evening's performances with the music. Merle Haggard and his band The Strangers, who had a western swing–style hit in 1980 with "I Think I'll Just Stay Here and Drink," also enjoy performing the music as often as they can. And as recently as 1995 George Strait had a hit with the tune "Right or Wrong," which was first covered by Emmett Miller and then Milton Brown, and soon became a western swing standard.

Though the name western swing evokes nostalgic images of cowboys with drums and trumpets packed on tour buses, the music itself remains a keystone to our nation's popular music. Its influence is far-reaching and can still be heard and seen in the music and images of today's country and rock and roll muscians.

Asleep at the Wheel

A deep appreciation for rural music brought three East Coast urbanites to Paw Paw, West Virginia, to become steeped in the music they so loved. During these formative years Ray Benson (b. 1951), Leroy Preston (b. 1951), and Reuben "Lucky Ocean" Gosfield (b.1951) were the three original members of the band. Soon after, however, a secretary named Chris O'Connell (b.1953) begged her way into the band and by doing so gave the band its prime balladeer.

A favorite with hippie fans of bluegrass and western swing, Asleep at the Wheel began opening for acts like Commander Cody and His Lost Planet Airmen and Poco. Joe Kerr, Commander Cody's manager, recommended that Asleep at the Wheel move to San Francisco after hearing the group, and in 1971 they did so. As one of the only "traditional" country bands in the city, they soon gathered a steady following. Floyd Domino was included on piano in February 1972, adding the crucial swing element to the band's sound.

Their first album, released in March 1973, included a cover of the Wills tune "Take Me Back to Tulsa." The response to the song made the band aware of the virtually untapped market during that time for western swing. Like many goat-ropers-turned-hippies

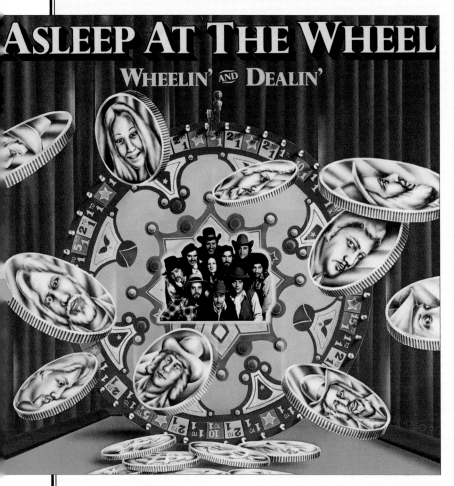

A nostalgic interest in the music made popular by men like Bob Wills and His Texas Playboys spawned a new generation of western swing-oriented bands during the 1970s. Perhaps the most successful of these groups, Asleep at the Wheel, blended Texas music of the 1940s with 1970s redneck rock.

Led by Philadelphia singer/guitarist Ray Benson, Asleep at the Wheel helped raise a new generation's consciousness to the music of Bob Wills. The group was the last to appear on stage with Wills in a mid-1970s televised concert on Austin City Limits.

the five core members moved in 1974 from their home away from home in San Francisco to the greener pastures of Austin, Texas, where they found their music was most appreciated. Another single, "Choo Choo Ch'Boogie," was embraced by radio and clubs alike, furthering the band's recognition around the country.

Two new members joined the band: Ed Vizard and Link Davis, Jr., the son of the highly acclaimed performer of "Big Mamou" and other popular Cajun and Texas songs. While Ed held down the rhythm as the band's new drummer, Link moved from fiddle to accordion and piano. Danny Levin, who'd been with the band in the West Virginia days, rejoined the group in Austin, but this time as fiddler and not pianist. These inclusions gave the band its ultimate western swing sound. As it had been popularized in the thirties and forties, western swing was now alive and well again in Texas.

Recommended Listening

Asleep at the Wheel. *Best of Asleep at the Wheel*. CEMA.
———. *The Swingin' Best*. Epic.
Bush, Johnny. *Fourteen Greatest Hits*. Power Play.
Gimble, Johnny. *Still Fiddlin' Around*. MCA.
Haggard, Merle. *A Tribute to the Best Damn Fiddle Player in the World (or My Salute to Bob Wills)*. Koch International.
Price, Ray. *San Antonio Rose: A Tribute to Bob Wills*. Koch International.
Thompson, Hank. *Vintage Collection*. Capitol.
Williams, Tex. *Vintage Collection*. Capitol.

Various. *Hillbilly Fever, Vol. 1: Legends of Western Swing*. Rhino.
———. *Okeh Western Swing*. Columbia Special Products.
———. *Texas Music, Vol. 2: Western Swing and Honkey Tonk*. Rhino.
Wills, Bob. *Anthology (1935–73)*. Rhino.
———. *The Essential Bob Wills*. Sony/Legacy.
———. *Tiffany Transcriptions, Vol. 2*. Rhino.
———. *Twenty-Four Greatest Hits*. Mercury.

Bibliography

Malone, Bill C. *Country Music USA* (second edition). Austin, Texas: University of Texas Press, 1985.

Ginell, Cary. *Milton Brown and the Founding of Western Swing*. Champaign, Illinois: University of Illinois Press, 1994.

Dunbar, Tom. *From Bob Wills to Ray Benson: A History of Western Swing* (volume 1). Austin, Texas: Term Publications, 1977.

Bekker, Jr. Peter O.E. *Country*. New York: Friedman/Fairfax Publishers, 1993.

Flint, Joe, and Judy Nelson. *The Insider's Country Music Handbook*. Salt Lake City, Utah: Gibb Smith Publishing, 1993.

Shestack, Melvin. *The Country Music Encyclopedia*. New York: Thomas Y. Crowell Company, 1974.

Photography Credits